TELLING tales in Latin

A New Latin Course and Storybook for Children

TELLING
Tales in Latin

A New Latin Course and Storybook for Children

by Lorna Robinson

Illustrated by Soham De

First published in 2013 by Souvenir Press
An imprint of Profile Books Ltd
3 Holford Yard, Bevin Way, London WC1X 9HD

Reprinted and Revised 2014

Reprinted 2018, 2021

ISBN 9780285641792

Typeset by M Rules

Printed and bound in Great Britain by Bell & Bain Ltd, Glasgow

I would like to dedicate this book to my brother Neil and my sister Marianne, for all the tales we told.   LR

I would like to dedicate this book to my parents and my friend Prachi, without whom this would not have been possible for me.   SD

Contents

Introduction

Vocabulary

A New Latin Course
and Storybook for Children

Introduction

Hello! My name is Ovid, and I lived in a city called "Roma" a very long time ago – over two thousand years ago, in fact, in the first century B.C. Back then, everyone in Roma spoke a language called Latin, and the Roman empire was a mighty one, spreading its ways and language to many countries all over the world.

I preferred not to take up arms in far-off places, but instead chose the life of a poet, spending my time in the bustling forum. This life turned out in the end to take me to a far off place after all, but that's another story.

My most famous poem was called "Metamorphoses" and in it I traced the world's history from the very beginning to my present time, through a chain of stories about things and people turning into other things!

I hope you'll enjoy exploring some of these magical stories, and learning the wonderful language I wrote them in as you go along. I also hope you don't mind me being your guide along the way.

in initio

So I am to tell these tales to you, which makes me the narrator of this little book. You might know the word narrator, but did you know that it comes from the Latin word "narro" which means "I tell a story"? The word for book is "liber", which gives us another common English word. Maybe you can guess what it might be.

I begin my tale with the very beginning of the world, when there was everything and nothing. By the way, it's all in Latin. You can't read Latin, you say? I think you'll find that by the end of this chapter you can. Go on, give it a go...

in initio est chaos. non est terra, non est aqua, non est
caelum. non est luna, non est sol.
aer, terra et oceanus sunt in una mole.

calor miscet cum frigido. lux miscet cum umbra.

tandem Natura separat undam, caelum et terram, et ponit
lunam et solem in caelo.

Words

So now you've met a little Latin. How many of these new words look like words you already know? Perhaps you could make a list of all the English words you know which look a bit like the Latin words in the passage. Can you work out the story?

Now you've had a go, here is what they mean:

aer = *air*	lux = *light*
aqua = *water*	miscet = *mixes*
caelo/caelum = *sky*	natura = *nature*
calor = *heat*	non = *not*
cum = *with*	oceanus = *ocean*
frigido = *the cold*	ponit = *places*
est = *there is*	separat = *separates*
et = *and*	sol = *sun*
in = *in*	sunt = *are*
in initio = *in the beginning*	tandem = *at last*
in una mole = *in one mass*	terra = *land*
luna = *moon*	umbra = *shadow*
	unda = *wave*

Did you get any right? There, I knew you would!

Word types

Just as Nature is separating things into different groups, let's split up the word types in the story into groups.

You may know that words for things are called "nouns", words for doing/being are "verbs", and words describing things are "adjectives". There is also a group of words called "prepositions", which tell you about where something is. These come before a noun and are words like "with", "in" and "on".

Can you write the Latin words and their English translations under the correct group headings?

Sentence practice

Here are some Latin sentences which describe how things might have been at the start of the world – I warn you now though, they're quite surreal! What's happening in them?

arbor est in caelo.
luna est in oceano.
aqua miscet cum igne.
sol est in terra.

arbor = *tree*
igne = *fire*

Can you think of any English words connected to these two new words? Write them down.

Activities

Well, there you go! Here we are at the end of the first chapter, and you've read some Latin, met some new words and learned what some Romans thought happened at the very beginning of the world. Not bad, eh?

What are the examples of metamorphosis which take place in this chapter?

My story might remind you of stories you've heard before. There are lots of different stories which explain the beginning of the world. Now scientists have made discoveries that give us a clearer idea of what happened at the start of the universe. In ancient times, though, people used their imaginations to make up stories instead.

Can you write your own version of what might have happened at the beginning of the world? You could make it an explosion of vivid colour and full of action, using lots of different adjectives and verbs! Or perhaps you have a completely different idea...

Primi humani

We Romans (or "Romani" in Latin!) borrowed lots of stories from our imaginative neighbours, the Greeks. One of the most famous stories we borrowed was about the ages of mankind. It told how, over time, we all became more and more careless of land and people, and how we polluted the seas too.

Have you ever heard someone tell you about "the good old days" and how things used to be much better years ago? Well, the story I'm about to tell is a little like that. Do you think things were much better in the past? Here's the story, so see what you think.

prima aetas est aurea. terra est communis. agri dant cibum
sponte sua. ver est aeternum.

secunda aetas est argentea. Iuppiter creat hiemem, aestatem,
et autumnum. iam feminae et viri habitant in villis.

tertia aetas est aenea. viri faciunt gladios et pugnant. iam sunt domini, dominae, servi et ancillae.

quarta aetas est ferrea. viri faciunt naves et visitant alteras terras. mercatores congerunt pecuniam.

Words

There are lots of new words in this story that you might be able to recognise. Perhaps you can have a look and take a guess at their meanings.

Right, here are the Latin translations of words to help you translate my little story! Words sometimes change their endings in Latin, so don't worry if the words look slightly different.

aenea = *bronze*

aetas = *age*

aestatem = *summer*

aeternum = *eternal*

agri = *fields*

alteras = *other*

ancillae = *slave-girls*

argentea = *silver*

aurea = *gold*

autumnum = *autumn*

cibum = *food*

communis = *communal*

congerunt = *pile up*

creat = *creates*

dant = give

dominae = *mistresses*

domini = *masters*

faciunt = *make*

feminae = *women*

ferrea = *iron*

gladios = *swords*

habitant = *live*

hiemem = *winter*

iam = *now*

in villis = *in houses*

Iuppiter = *Jupiter*

mercatores = *merchants*

naves = *ships*

pecuniam = *money*

prima = *first*

pugnant = *fight*

secunda = *second*

servi = *slaves*

sponte sua = *on their own*

sunt = *are*

tertia = *third*

quarta = *fourth*

ver = *spring*

viri = *men*

visitant = *visit*

Verbs

Verbs, as I mentioned in the last chapter, are "doing" words. There are lots of verbs in this story, as people are very busy doing all sorts of things. Can you find the verbs in the passage and write down the Latin and English? Once you've done this, write down in brackets next to the Latin verb how many people are doing the action. What do you notice?

Yes, that's right! Verbs in Latin involving one person doing something end in "t", whereas verbs involving more than one person doing the action end in "nt". Here are two examples:

pugnat - *he/she fights*
pugnant - *they fight*

est - *he/she/it is*
sunt - *they are*

Verbs involving one person are called **singular** verbs and those involving more than one person are called **plural** verbs.

Using what you have just learnt, can you turn the following plural Latin verbs into singular verbs?

1. visitant
2. creant
3. habitant

And can you turn these ones into plural verbs?

1. ridet (*laughs*)
2. laudat (*praises*)
3. portat (*carries*)

Have a go at these Latin sentences, which are examples of some of the things people got up to in the first four ages of mankind from the story. Can you guess which age each sentence is describing?

1. feminae visitant alteras terras.
2. viri sunt laeti.
3. feminae et viri habitant in agris.
4. viri sunt irati.

laeti = *happy*
irati = *angry*

Activities

Here are a few little activities for you to explore before we leave this story behind and go on to the next tale...

As you can see, a series of pictures is a vivid way to illustrate the four ages of mankind described in the story. Many people in the past have drawn their own versions and added their own details. You might have your own ideas about what sort of images would best tell the tale! You could write it with captions to make a comic strip if you like.

Another way of telling the story might be a short play about one of the ages of mankind. You'd need a narrator (like me!), and a couple of characters. Which age would you choose? And what props might you need?

You could even have a go at inventing a whole new age of mankind and write an account of what it might be like – this always tempted me! Would people be happy or sad? What would they be doing, and what would the world look like? One of things I love about inventing stories is that you can be as detailed and imaginative as you want – it's your world and you can fill it with all kinds of things! What will you call your new age?

See you in the next story.

tres.
II

Diluvium.

Do you remember what the iron age people were like in our last story? Well, it got to the point where Jupiter, the powerful king of the gods, decided that humans had become too wicked. What do you think he did?

He decided to ask his brother Neptune, who was in charge of the oceans, to help him flood the entire world! Here is how it happened, so they say...

Iuppiter est iratissimus. Notum mittit. Notus liquidis alis volat. liquidam barbam habet. aqua de capillis fluit. imber in agros fundit. rivi arbores et villas et greges carpunt.

Before you have a go at translating the Latin, as always, see if you can guess some of the new words here from English words you know.

Had a go? Here are some Latin words to help you too!

barba = *beard*
carpunt = *seize*
de capillis = *down from his hair*

fluit = *flows*
fundit = *pours*
grex = *flock*
habet = *has*
imber = *rain*

in agros = *onto fields*
iratissimus = *very angry*
liquidis alis = *with watery wings*

mittit = *sends*
Notus = *South wind*
rivus = *river*
volat = *flies*

Remember that words often change their endings in Latin, so you need to look for a Latin word that is similar sometimes in the list rather than exactly the same. You'll notice something different about this chapter and all chapters from now on. This is that the verbs usually go at the end of the sentence. Isn't that strange! So you might wonder how you know who is doing what in a sentence... The Latin word "in" can mean "in" or "on", but if it is followed by a noun with an object ending, it means "into" or "onto". What's an object ending, you say? Well, find out below!

Nouns

We saw last time how verbs change to show how many people are doing the action. Can you remember what the singular and plural endings are? For practice, you could find all the verbs in the passage above and write them down, saying whether they are singular or plural.

In this chapter, we are looking at noun endings. Have a look at these:

1 (f)	2 (m)	2 (n)	3 (m)
barba	Notus	templum (*temple*)	clamor (*shout*)
barbam	Notum	templum	clamorem
barbae	Noti	templa	clamores
barbas	Notos	templa	clamores

There are four different endings for each group! Can you guess what each ending tells you?

Nouns in Latin are put into groups according to their endings. Nouns that end in -a are usually in group 1 and are usually feminine. This is shown by the (f) - yes, even objects are said to have a gender in Latin! Nouns ending in -us or -um are usually group 2 and are usually either masculine (m) or neuter (n), and group 3 nouns are quite different! The only real way of knowing what group a noun is in is by learning it, so from now on, I'll put the group number in brackets in the vocabulary lists.

Now for the meaning of those endings. Have a look at these two sentences from the passage

1. Notus liquidis alis volat.
2. Notum mittit.

"Notus" and "Notum" both appear, but in the first sentence he is the subject, and in the second, he is the object. When nouns are the object in a sentence, they often end in -m (apart from neuter nouns which don't change at all!). When there is more than one of the noun, then the endings change again - so Notus (south wind) would become Noti, (south winds), and Notum, the south wind as object, would become Notos (south winds). 'barba' would behave differently, as you can see from the chart above!

Have a go at turning these nouns, which are singular subjects, into plural subjects:

barba
oceanus
amicus

And can you turn these plural objects into singular objects?

lunas
terras
tabernas

amicus (2) = *friend*
taberna (1) = *shop*

Let's carry on with our story. Remember to look out for all the things we have just learned about!

iam non est terra, modo oceanus. puella in colle sedet. puer in arbore sedet et pisces captat! sub aqua, Nereides urbes vident. pisces per fenestras et ianuas natant.

captat = *catches*	natant = *swim*	puella (1) = *girl*
ianua (1) = *door*	Nereis (3) = *sea*	puer (2) = *boy*
in arbore = *in a*	*nymph*	sedet = *sits*
tree	per fenestras =	sub = *under*
in colle = *on a hill*	*through windows*	urbs (3) = *city*
modo = *only*	piscis (3) = *fish*	vident = *see*

Activities

In my poem I enjoyed writing speeches by the gods, and I included lots of them! I wonder what Jupiter would say if he were telling the sky and the sea to flood the world! I suppose he would need to use lots of persuasive words. Why should they flood the world? What sort of arguments might work to persuade them? How do you think Jupiter might speak? You can make your writing sound like his voice. Would it be calm and serious? Would it be angry and frightening?

Perhaps you can write your own speech and give it to your friends, family and classmates. Maybe some other people could write speeches persuading the sea and sky not to flood the world. Is it fair to flood the world? Read the speeches, for and against, then people can ask questions. I love a bit of debating!

My favourite bit of the tale is the weird underwater world that was created by the flood. I could have written a whole poem about the world under the sea, which the Nereids could see! Imagine all the wonderful things they might find as they swim around. Could you write from the perspective of a sea nymph who has never seen cities and houses before? They might have different words to describe things they see. You'd need to put yourself in their minds, and make the poem descriptive and detailed. Perhaps you can even illustrate your poem.

Why do you think there are so many stories about floods in societies all over the world?

quattuor IV

Deucalion et Pyrrha

So now to the next part of my story, where we meet a rather sorry little bird trying to find a place to land in a world without land.

avis fessa, diu terram quaerens, tandem in oceano cadit. post multos dies, aqua paulatim subsidit. ecce! iam terra apparet. modo unus vir et una femina supersunt in rate. vir, nomine Deucalion, est bonus. femina, nomine Pyrrha, est bona. Deucalion et Pyrrha sunt soli, et igitur orant.

Can you pick out all the nouns in the passage, and split them into two groups – ones that are subjects and ones that are objects. Remember that in Latin you can do this even without translating the sentences, because the endings show us the answers. Clever, isn't it?!

All done? Well, here are some words to help you read the story. As usual, don't forget to look for English words which are similar to the Latin words. How many can you find?

apparet = *appears*	orant = *pray*
avis (3) = *bird*	paulatim = *little by little*
bonus/bona = *good*	
	post multos dies = *after*
cadit = *falls*	*many days*
diu = *for a long time*	quaerens = *seeking*
ecce! = *look!*	quod = *because*
fessa = *tired*	soli = *alone*
igitur = *therefore*	subsidit = *subsides*
in rate = *in a boat*	supersunt = *remain*
nomine = *called*	unus/una = *one*

You'll see that I've included a number next to the words to show what group the nouns are in.

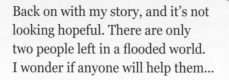

Back on with my story, and it's not looking hopeful. There are only two people left in a flooded world. I wonder if anyone will help them...

dea Themis virum et feminam audit. dicit "lapides post terga iacite!". Deucalion et Pyrrha sunt solliciti, sed lapides iaciunt. subito lapides mollire et ducere novas formas incipiunt. brevi tempore lapides sunt viri et feminae! tandem Deucalion et Pyrrha sunt laeti.

Here are some more words:

audit = *hears*
brevi tempore = *in a short time*
dea (1) = *goddess*
dicit = *says*

incipiunt = *begin*
lapis (3) = *stone*
mollire = *to soften*
novas = *new*

ducere = *to take on*
forma (1) = *shape*
iacite = *throw!*
iaciunt = *throw*

post terga = *behind your backs*
subito = *suddenly*
solliciti = *worried*

You might have noticed that there are lots of words describing things in these two passages, words which we call adjectives. Can you find them all?

What do you notice? Let's have a closer look. Here's a sentence from the passage:

vir, nomine Deucalion, est bonus. femina, nomine Pyrrha, est bona.

"bonus" and "bona" both mean "good" but the word changes to agree with the gender of the word it is describing. Can you find any other examples of this in the two passages? You might also notice that when an adjective is describing Deucalion and Pyrrha together, such as "soli" meaning "alone", then it becomes plural. You could have a go at changing these adjectives to make them agree.

sollicitus, bonus, solus.

1. .... dea
2. .... vir
3. .... vir et femina
4. .... puella

The three adjectives above behave like nouns in group 1 (like puella) and 2 (like vir).

There are actually a few examples of metamorphosis in this chapter. How many different examples of things changing into other things can you find?

At the beginning, we met a poor little bird who couldn't find anywhere to land. Have a go at writing an account of the flooding of the world from the perspective of an animal. Which animal will you choose? Imagine what particular problems your animal will face, and how they will experience this new world.

Part of the story involved stones changing into humans! That's pretty amazing, but there are actually a number of stories from societies all round the world about stones changing into living things – I've told a fair few others myself in my time! Why do you think there are lots of stories like this?

We've met the word "lapis" (stone), "lapides" (stones), but there are other words in Latin for stones. There is "saxum" (rock) and "calculus" (pebble). Can you think of any English words that come from any of these three words? Some you might guess quickly, others might come from looking at a dictionary.

Finally, we saw how adjectives change in Latin to agree
with what they describe. Are there any examples of this
ever happening in English?

See you in the next story.

quinque
V

Apollo et Daphne

You might have the impression from my stories so far that the gods are a very grand and serious lot, always making judgements on good and bad behaviour, organising the world, and being responsible. Well, one thing's for sure, even the mightiest and most powerful gods get themselves into all kinds of scrapes. Here's a tale about the god Apollo, a mighty archer, god of healing, medicine, philosophy and more. It all begins after Apollo insults a lively young lad called Cupid...

Cupido, iratissimus, ex pharetra duas sagittas carpit. aurea sagitta amorem facit, plumbea sagitta amorem delet. Cupido plumbeam sagittam in nympha figit, et auream sagittam in Apollone figit.

statim Apollo nympham amat, sed nympha currit. deus clamat "nympha, mane! non ego sum agricola, non greges observo. Iuppiter est meus pater!"

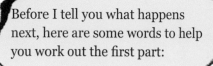

Before I tell you what happens next, here are some words to help you work out the first part:

amat = *loves*
amor (3) = *love*
currit = *runs*

delet = *destroys*
duas = *two*
ego = *I*

figit = *strikes*
grex (3) = *flock*
meus/a = *my*

nympha (1) = *nymph*
observo = *I watch*

pater (3) = *father*
ex pharetra (1) = *out of a quiver*
plumbeus/a = *lead*

sagitta (1) = *arrow*
sed = *but*
sum = *I am*

Remember last time we looked at adjectives? Can you pick out all the adjectives in this passage?

Verbs

This chapter introduces something very strange and interesting about Latin verbs! You already know that the ending "t" on a verb means "he/she" does the verb, and "nt" means "they", so "delet" means "he destroys" and "delent" means "they destroy". If you pick out all the verbs in the story, what do you notice?

That's right! There are lots of different endings, and they depend on which group the verb belongs to. In fact, here are all the endings for the verbs in each verb group:

group 1
amo = *I love*
amas = *you love*
amat = *he/she loves*

amamus = *we love*
amatis = *you (plural) love*
amant = *they love*

amare = *to love*
(this is called the 'infinitive')

group 2
deleo = *I destroy*
deles = *you destroy*
delet = *he/she destroys*

delemus = *we destroy*
deletis = *you destroy*
delent = *they destroy*

delere = *to destroy*

group 3
mitto = *I send*
mittis = *you send*
mittit = *he/she sends*

mittimus = *we send*
mittitis = *you send*
mittunt = *they send*

mittere = *to send*

group 4
audio = *I hear*
audis = *you hear*
audit = *he/she hears*

audimus = *we hear*
auditis = *you hear*
audiunt = *they hear*

audire = *to hear*

By the way, some verbs in group 3 can look a bit like group 4 verbs, such as "facio" which means "I do/make". Perhaps you can keep an eye out for these! Phew! That all seems a lot to take in, but don't worry too much for now. In days gone by, classes of children would chant these words to remember them. You're welcome to have a go at that if you like! But for now, have a look at each group and spot what is different about each group.

On with our story . . .

Daphne currit. aura capillos retro impellit. nympha,
perterrita, clamat "fer opem, pater!".
subito corpus est grave. capilli in frondes crescunt,
lacerti in ramos mutant. pedes radicibus haerent. nympha
est laurus! Apollo arborem quoque amat.
deus dicit "non es coniunx, sed iam es mea arbor!".

Here are some more words:

aura (1) = *breeze*	grave = *heavy*	laurus (2) = *laurel tree*
capilli (2) = *hair*	haerent (2) = *stick*	mutant (1) = *change*
clamat (1) = *shouts*	hanc = *her/it*	opis (3) = *help*
coniunx (3) = *wife/ husband*	impellit (3) = *drives* in frondes = *into leaves*	pedes (3) = *feet* perterritus/a = *terrified*
corpus (3) = *body*		
crescit (3) = *grows*	in ramos = *into branches*	quoque = *also*
es = *you are*		radicibus = *in roots*
fer = *bring*	lacerti (2) = *arms*	retro = *backwards*

You'll see I've now included in the word list which group the verb is in. I will do this from now on. Perhaps you can have a go at these practice sentences to help you get used to the verb groups.

Translate the following verbs:

1. delemus
2. crescitis
3. curris
4. haerent
5. amat
6. exspecto ((1) *wait for*)

Just to make life awkward, as well as verbs which fit into the four groups above, there are some verbs which insist on misbehaving and doing their own thing! We call these irregular verbs, although I prefer to call them "wild" verbs! Two of the most common ones are the ones below:

sum = *I am*	possum = *I can*
es = *you are*	potes = *you can*
est = *he/she/it is*	potest = *he/she can*
sumus = *we are*	possumus = *we can*
estis = *you are*	potestis = *you can*
sunt = *they are*	possunt = *they can*
esse = *to be*	posse = *to be able*

Activities

Did you notice how my tale explained the process of Daphne becoming a tree? First, her hair, then her arms changed, then her feet... Often in fairy stories, magical events are passed over, but in my story, I have described the magical happening in detail. Why do you think fairy stories usually avoid describing magical things, but just state that they happened? What effect does it have when someone describes it in detail? Have a think about this, or perhaps a discussion with friends or your class.

Pick a magical event from a favourite story or make up your own. Now can you describe the event in detail as if you were writing up a scientific experiment? It needs to be impersonal and objective (look these words up if you're unsure what they mean). Think about the style and content of your document.

I have always thought that my stories would make great comic strips – I like to focus on visual detail like the nymph's streaming hair in this chapter. Can you turn this story into a comic strip by picking some vivid images and using these to tell the story?

Was it helpful for Daphne to turn into a tree? Do you think it was her father who changed her, or was it something else? Perhaps you think you can make up a better ending than I did! Well, why don't you have a go!

The moment of Daphne turning into a tree has captured the imaginations of artists, writers and sculptors. Why do you think it has been so inspiring?

I'll leave you with that thought!

Phaethon et Sol

We've all ignored advice from teachers, parents, friends and emperors. It's so tempting to have a go at something, isn't it? Here's a story about one young lad, Phaethon, who thought he could try his hand at controlling something extremely powerful. The word "sol" might be a clue.

Phaethon est filius Solis, sed puer, nomine Ephaphus, inquit
"tu es stultus! non es filius Solis".

Phaethon, iratus, in caelum ascendit, et candidam regiam Solis
advenit.

ibi Sol filium salutat, et eum intra invitat.

Phaethon rogat "esne mihi pater?"

Sol inquit "ita vero! ullum donum tibi do".

Phaethon rogat "currumne tuum hodie agere possum?"

Sol inquit "necesse est mihi te sinere. sed est periculosum iter.
esne certus?"

"ita vero!" Phaethon exclamat.

"deinde audi diligenter. prima via est ardua.
medio caelo via est altissima. ego ipse videre oceanum et terras
timeo. ultima via est prona. cave!"

Words

You might notice a couple of extra letters have become attached to some words here and there. Can you spot what those letters are, and what they might mean?

While you are having a think about that, here are some useful words for you:

advenio (4) = *I arrive at, meet*
altissimus/a = *highest*
arduus/a = *steep*

ascendo (3) = *I climb*
audi = *listen!*
candidus/a = *gleaming white*

cave = *beware!*
certus/a = *certain*
currus (4) = *chariot*

deinde = *then*
diligenter = *carefully*
do (1) = *I give*
donum (2) = *gift*

eum = *him*
filius (2) = *son*
hodie = *today*
ibi = *there*
inquit = *says*

intra = *inside*
invito (1) = *I invite*
ipse = *myself*
ita vero = *yes*
iter (3) = *journey*

medio caelo = *in the middle of the sky*
mihi = *to/for me*

necesse = *necessary*
periculosus/a = *dangerous*

pronus/a = *facing downwards*
regia (1) = *palace*
rogo (1) = *I ask*
saluto (1) = *I greet*
sino (3) = *I allow*

stultus/a = *stupid*
tibi = *to/for you*
timeo (2) = *I am afraid*
tu = *you*

tuus/a = *your*
ullus/a = *any*
ultimus/a = *last*
via (1) = *path*

So, did you work out what those two sneaky little letters were? And why they were there? The letters are "ne" and the reason they are there is that they show a question is being asked. We didn't have question marks in those days, you see.

Have a look at these two sentences:

"sum tibi pater" = *I am your father.*
"sumne tibi pater" = *Am I your father?*

The "ne" always appears on the end of the first word in the sentence. It's not there in questions which have question words, such as "where" or "why" because these already signpost that it is a question.

And now to the next part of my story!

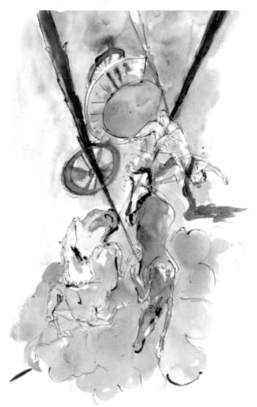

Phaethon adhuc currum cupit. pater filium ad candidum currum ducit. axis est aureus et temo est aureus! rotae sunt aureae et radii sunt argentei.

fortis Phaethon in curro ascendit, et tenere habenas gaudet. postquam Aurora advenit, equi per caelum currunt.

Phaethon tenere habenas non potest. mox equi viam relinquunt. Phaethon est perterritus!

tum magnae urbes in cinerem vertunt. silvae cum montibus ardent. puer omnem orbem accensum videt.

tandem Iuppiter fulmen in puerum mittit. Phaethon praeceps de caelo cadit.

Words

Here are some more words:

accensus/a = *burnt*
adhuc = still
ardeo (2) = *I burn*

Aurora = *the goddess Dawn*
axis (3) = *axle*
cado (3) = *I fall*

cinis (3) = ash
cum montibus = *with mountains*
cupio (4) = *I desire*

de caelo = *down from the sky*
duco (3) = *I lead*
equus (2) = *horse*

fortis/e = *brave*
fulmen (3) = *thunderbolt*
gaudeo (2) = *I enjoy*

gens (3) = *people*
habenae (1) = *reins*
magnus/a = *large*

mox = *soon*
omnis/e = *all*
postquam = *after*

praeceps = *headlong*
radius (2) = *spoke (of wheel)*
relinquo (3) = *I leave*
rota (1) = *wheel*

scio (4) = *I know*
silva (1) = *wood*
temo (3) = *pole*
teneo (2) = *I hold*

tum = *then*
verto (3) = *I turn*

 Activities

As you have seen, Jupiter decides to step in when things get really out of hand. It seems quite cruel to have struck poor, frightened Phaethon out of the sky. What would you have done?

The palace of Sol, the Sun is a beautiful, gleaming white place, isn't it? I loved describing it in my story, and used lots of words for light and sparkle. Maybe you could have a go at describing a palace of the Sun, and see if you can find even more words in English for shining and shimmering light!

What is the metamorphosis which take place in this story? It's a bit more difficult to spot than the ones we've met so far, but it is there.
Many people have seen this tale this as a little moral fable, warning boys and girls not to ignore advice from their parents!

Well, let's move on, shall we, because if you think
this lad made a mistake, see what you think of the
young man in my next story!

Echo et Narcissus

We humans are naturally fascinated with ourselves. It's a way of understanding our world. The problem is that you can get so wrapped up in yourself that strange and terrible things can happen! This brings me to a tale about a very well-known youngster called Narcissus...

multae puellae Narcissum cupiunt. sed Narcissus nullas
puellas amat, quod magnam superbiam habet. saepe
Narcissum videt Echo. Echo adhuc corpus habet, sed
non vocem habet. illa modo repetere verba potest.
Narcissus, solus in silva, inquit "quis adest?" et "adest"
respondet Echo. Narcissus stupet! clamat "veni!" et
"veni!" respondet Echo.

Words

Here are words to help you with this first part of the story:

adsum = *I am here*	saepe = *often*
ille/illa = *he/she*	sibi = *to/for him*
multus/a = *many*	stupeo (2) = *I am stupefied*
nullus/a = *no*	superbia (1) = *pride*
quis = *who*	veni = *come!*
repeto (3) = *I repeat*	verbum (2) = *word*
respondeo (2) = *I reply*	vox (3) = *voice*

Did you spot the question? But there weren't any "ne"s tagged on to the end of words, were there? That's because the question had a question word, in this case "quis".

Let's continue with our sorry little tale...

Echo ad Narcissum currit. Narcissus clamat "abi!" et "abi" respondet Echo. Narcissus currit. Echo, maesta, in cavernis celat. paulatim corpus in saxum mutat. modo vox superest.

Narcissus, fessus, prope fontem sedet. cenam et vinum consumit. tum in aquam liquidam spectat. statim mirabilem imaginem videt. Narcissus stupet! sua lumina, suos pulchros capillos spectat. ubi aquam tangit, imago evanescit. "cur me fugis?" clamat Narcissus, et ibi semper manet. tandem nymphae croceum florem cum albis foliis inveniunt. post mortem quoque, Narcissus adhuc in Stygiam aquam spectat.

Words

And here are those vital words to help you
unlock the rest of the story:

abi! = *go away!*
caverna (1) = *cave*
cena (1) = *dinner*
celo (1) = *I hide*

consumo (3) = *I eat*
croceus/a = *yellow*
cum albis foliis = *with white
petals*
cur = *why*

evanesco (3) = *I vanish*
flos (3) = *flower*
imago (3) = *image*
in Stygia aqua = *in the Stygian
water*

liquidus/a = *clear*
lumina (3) = *eyes*

maneo (2) = *I stay*
mirabilis/e = *wonderful*
post mortem = *after death*
prope fontem = *near a
spring*

semper = *always*
specto (1) = *I look at*
statim = *straightaway*
Stygius/a = *of the River Styx*
supersum = *I survive,
remain*

suus/a = *his, her, its*
tamen = *however*
tango (3) = *I touch*

ubi = *when/where*
vinum (2) = *wine*

Well, at least he got to carry on admiring himself!

We've already seen that nouns (words for things) change their endings depending on whether the word is a subject or an object in the sentence. Nouns also have a different ending to show that the subject is doing something "to" or "for" the noun in question. This ending is called the "dative" ending. Have a look at the table below to see what I mean:

Group 1	Group 2	Group 3
aqua (*water*)	amicus (*friend*)	arbor (*tree*)
aquam (*water*)	amicum (*friend*)	arborem (*tree*)
aquae (*to/for water*)	amico (*to/for the friend*)	arbori (*to/for the tree*)
		arbores (*trees*)
aquae (*waters*)	amici (*friends*)	arbores (*trees*)
aquas (*waters*)	amicos (*friends*)	arboribus (*to/for the trees*)
aquis (*to/for waters*)	amicis (*to/for the friends*)	

Here's an example of the dative being used in an English

The boy gave a present to his friend.
In this sentence "to his friend" would be in the dative case if it were in Latin, and we call this the "indirect object".

Have a go at translating these words:
1. saxo
2. puellis
3. flori

And have a go at putting these words into Latin:
1. to the stones
2. for the girl
3. to the flowers

Activities

As is often the case in my stories, there is more than one instance of metamorphosis in this chapter. Can you find all the examples of metamorphoses?

One of the things I like to do when telling stories is to put in little hints and clues about the theme of the story as I go along. Maybe you can spot some examples of how I might have done this in the story I have just told? Look carefully at my sentences and the words I have used, and even what order I have put them in. See if you can spot any favourite techniques of mine!

This little tale is perfect for producing a play. Why don't you have a go at writing a play script based on some or all of the events you've just read about and maybe even act it out to an audience?

This is yet another story which could be said to contain a moral. What is the moral do you think, and is there more than one?

The story explains in a mythological way where echoes come from. Obviously you might prefer the more traditional explanation, but it does make a rather charming story don't you think? You could have a go at inventing your own story about why something came to be. Pick anything you like and have a go!

On we go to the next tale...

Arachne

I've been told I'm rather good at writing, but I wouldn't want to show off! No-one likes a show-off, after all. But actually, that's not the only reason not to show off. It turns out that those powerful gods can get quite jealous of human skill, and it seems that there's nothing they like better than to take revenge on us.

A girl called Arachne learned that the hard way...

olim erat puella, nomine Arachne. nomen memorabile
quaerebat, quamvis in villa parva habitabat. Arachne
in suo horto tegebat, et nymphae laborem mirabilem
spectabant.

puella rudem lanam in orbes glomerabat. tum lanam
molliebat, et pollice fusum vertebat. dicebat tamen
"mea mater non erat mihi magister. nec Athena me
docebat".

Words

Before I give you these words, I should warn you to watch out for some new verb endings which might make it tricky to pair up the verbs in the passage with the ones in the list below! Try to look at the first few letters to help you out. All will be revealed soon, but do feel free to take a guess at what these new endings might mean.

doceo (2) = *I teach*
parvus/a = *small*

erat = *was*
fusus (2) = *spindle*
glomero (1) = *I gather together*

hortus (2) = *garden*
lana (1) = *wool*
memorabilis/e = *memorable*
mollio (4) = *I soften*

labor (3) = *work*

magister (2) = *teacher*
mater (3) = *mother*
nec = *nor*
olim = *once*
orbis (3) = *ball*
pollice = *with her thumb*
quamvis = *although*

quaero (3) = *I seek*
rudis/e = *rough*
specto (1) = *I look at*
tego (3) = *I weave*

So let's have a look at those endings now:

habitabat *came from* habito
quaerebat *came from* quaero
docebat *came from* doceo

As you can see, the word has changed quite a lot. Have you guessed why? Yes, I have introduced you to a new "tense". A tense of a verb tells you when the action happens. So far you have met the present tense, so all the verb endings you know describe actions which happen right now. But the new verb endings in this story are from a past tense, called the imperfect tense. So words such as "habitabat" and "dicebat" describe actions which go on for a while in the past (for example "she used to live there" and "she was saying to her friend"). Here are the endings for each person:

amabam	*I was loving*
amabas	*You were loving*
amabat	*He/she/it was loving*
amabamus	*We were loving*
amabatis	*You were loving*
amabant	*They were loving*

Right, we have a story to finish! Back to our talented seamstress Arachne. Have you guessed what happens to her?

Athena anum simulabat. falsos canos in caput addebat, et
infirmum corpus baculo sustinebat.
tum dicebat "noli spernere meum consilium. cede deae,
temeraria puella". Arachne, irata, dicebat "cur non ipsa
venit?".

tum dea dicebat "venio!" et formam removebat. erat
Athena! puella sola non erat territa. Athena et Arachne
telas constituebant et tegebant.

Athena scopulum Mavortis pingebat.

Arachne Europam et alteras fabulas pingebat.

Arachne erat victor! Athena, iratissima, laborem rumpebat,
et puellam percutiebat. Arachne erat perterrita. Athena
herbas spargebat, et statim capilli, naso et aures Arachnes
cadebant. caput erat subito minimum, et tum omne corpus
quoque. digiti in latere haerebant! cetera erat venter, de quo
puella stamen emittebat. Arachne adhuc tegebat, aranea.

Hmm,"aranea"... What do you think that is?
Before I give you the rest of the words, perhaps
you can find all the verbs in this section and
translate them.

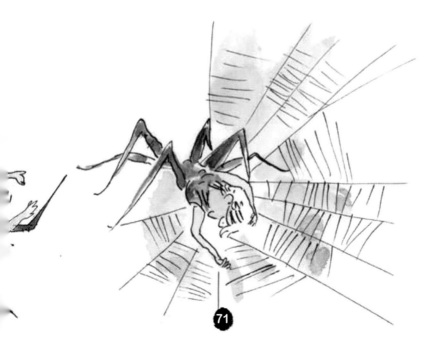

Words

Right, here are those words!

addo (3) = *I add*
alterus/a = *other*
anus (2) = *old woman*
Arachnes = *of Arachne*

aranea (1) = *spider*
aures (3) = *ears*
baculo = *with a stick*

cani (2) = *white hair*
caput (3) = *head*
cede = *concede*
ceterus/a = *the rest*

consilium (2) = *advice*
constituo (3) = *I set up*
de quo = *from which*
emitto (3) = *I send out*

fabula (1) = *story*
falsus/a = *false*
fama (1) = *fame*
herba (1) = *grass*

infirmus/a = *shaky*
in latere = *in her side*
ipse/a = *himself/herself/
 itself*

Mavortis = *of Mars*
minimus/a = *very small*
naso (3) = *nose*
noli spernere = *don't ignore*

pingo (3) = *I create a picture
 of*
percutio (3) = *I hit*
removeo (2) = *I remove*

scopulum (2) = *rock*
simulo (1) = *I pretend to be*
spargo (3) = *I scatter*

stamen (3) = *thread*
tela (1) = *loom*
temerarius/a = *rash*
venter (3) = *stomach*
victor (3) = *winner*

See how the imperfect tense has changed the verbs?
You'll get used to the way that these verbs behave.
Have a go at translating these:

parabat   (*from* paro (1) = *I prepare*)
monebant   (*from* moneo (2) = *I warn*)
scribebamus (*from* scribo (3) = *I write*)
audiebatis   (*from* audio (4) = *I hear*)

Activities

What are the examples of metamorphosis in this tale?

It's another example of a story which explains the origin of something, in this case the origin of spiders and why they like making beautiful webs! Can you think of any other purposes this story might have?

Arachne and Athena both weave stories about the gods, but they both tell very different tales. How do the two stories they have chosen represent the gods and what does the choice of story tell you about the storyteller?

Why don't you pick a subject and come up with two very different stories to describe it? It could be two pictures of the same thing from different perspectives, or two poems, or even two different newspaper stories? There are all kinds of different ways of telling about one thing, which is sort of what my little book is all about!

So, on to the next tale...

novem
IX

Daedalus

There once was a very clever but troubled inventor called Daedalus. Trapped on the island of Crete by the powerful king Minos, he was miserable and homesick. When Minos' wife fell in love with a bull (yes, a bull!), she gave birth to the terrible Minotaur, a half-man, half-bull, which ate human flesh. Minos then told Daedalus to build a prison for the monster.

Daedalus labyrinthum aedificavit. multas vias creavit
et notas turbavit. lumina in errorem duxit. est
rivus, nomine Maeandrus, qui fluit et refluit. qualis
Maeandrus in liquidis undis ludit, ita Daedalus
innumeras vias creavit, et vix ipse revertere ad ianuam
poterat! Minos monstrum intra servavit.

Ariadne erat filia regis. ubi Theseum spectavit, eum
amavit. Ariadne filum Theseo dedit. tum Theseus
labyrinthum intravit et monstrum vicit. ianuam iterum
filo invenit.

You may have noticed that the verbs in this passage look
different again! That's because I'm introducing you to another
past tense, called the perfect tense. I've translated the "perfect"
verbs below for you and given which verb group they are from.
The perfect tense is a little bit more complicated than the
imperfect, but nothing to worry about.

Words

Right, now for those words:

aedificavit *from* aedifico (1) = *he built*
creavit *from* creo (1) = *he created*
dedit *from* do (1) = *he gave*
duxit *from* duco (3) = *he led*

error (3) = *error*
Filia (1) = *daughter*
Filo = *with the thread*
filum (2) = *thread*
Fluo = *I flow*

innumerus/a = *countless*
ita = *in this way*
iterum = *again*

intravit *from* intro (1) = *he entered*
invenit *from* invenio (4) = *he found*

labyrinthus (2) = maze
ludo (3) = I play
Maeandrus (2) = Maeander
nota (1) = sign

poterat = he was able
qualis = just like
qui = which

refluo (3) = I flow back
regis = of the king
reverto (3) = *I return*
servavit *from* servo (1) = *he kept*
spectavit *from* specto (1) = *she saw*

turbavit from turbo (1) = he mixed up
vicit from vinco (3) = he defeated
vix = scarcely

You may not have heard of the river Maeander, but in my time, this river, which was said to flow past Troy, was famous for its winding ways. This is where we get the word "meander" from. In this part of the story, I've compared the complexity of the labyrinth to the winding ways of the river. Can you see how the river and the maze are similar? In fact, this sort of comparison is called a "simile"!

Now let's have a look at those new perfect endings:

creavit *came from* creo (1)
duxit *came from* duco (3)
vicit *came from* vinco (3)
aedificavit *came from* aedifico (1)

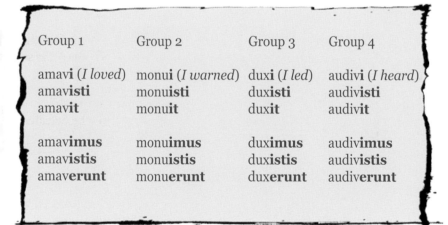

As you can see, the word has changed quite a lot! The perfect tense describes actions which happened once and then are finished (for example "she taught" and "she has looked for").

Here are the endings for each person:

Group 1	Group 2	Group 3	Group 4
ama**vi** (*I loved*)	monu**i** (*I warned*)	dux**i** (*I led*)	audi**vi** (*I heard*)
ama**visti**	monu**isti**	dux**isti**	audi**visti**
ama**vit**	monu**it**	dux**it**	audi**vit**
ama**vimus**	monu**imus**	dux**imus**	audi**vimus**
ama**vistis**	monu**istis**	dux**istis**	audi**vistis**
ama**verunt**	monu**erunt**	dux**erunt**	audi**verunt**

At the moment, the key thing is to recognise the perfect tense and be able to work out which verb it comes from. The rest can wait until later, as we have a story to finish!

As it's not over for Daedalus. Not by a long shot...

Daedalus interea Creten et longum exilium oderat. igitur in ordine pennas posuit. pennas filo et cera ligavit. erat qualis vera avis. puer Icarus prope patrem stabat. pennas captabat, ceram pollice molliebat. tandem Daedalus laborem finivit, et oscula filio dedit.

tum volabant! pastor et arator cum plaustro
subter stabant, et stipuerunt. sed Icarus prope
solem volabat. cerae tabescebant! puer nudos
lacertos quatiebat. clamavit "pater!" et in
oceanum cecidit.

Words

> What a sad story for the talented inventor and his over-ambitious young son. It reminds me of another story in this book...

arator (3) = *ploughman*
cecidit *from cado* (3) = *I fall*
cera (1) = *wax*
cum plaustro = *with his wagon*

eas = *them*
exclamavit *from exclamo* (1) = *he called out*
exilium (2) = *exile*

filo et cera = *with wax and thread*
finivit *from* finio (4) = *he finished*
in ordine = *in order*

longus/a = *long*
ligavit *from* ligo (1) = *he tied*
nudus/a = *bare*
oderat = *he hated*

osculum (2) = *kiss*
pastor (3) = *shepherd*
penna (1) = *feather*

posuit *from* pono (3) = *he put*
prope patrem = *near his father*

prope solem = *near the sun*
quatio (4) = *I shake*
sto (1) = *I stand*
stipuerunt *from* stupeo (2) = *they were dumbfounded*

subter = *underneath*
tabesco (3) = *I melt*
verus/a = *true*

I've put in the translations for the perfect verbs again, rather than just giving you the first person present tense – you will get used to which perfect ending is from which verb – it just takes a bit of practice! Like learning to fly...

And speaking of practice, can you have a go at translating these perfect verbs?

1. ligavimus
2. dederunt
3. finivi
4. posuistis
5. stipuit
6. duxisti

Activities

What are the metamorphoses in this story? They don't necessarily have to have happened inside the story. Sometimes I just refer to them!

Daedalus was a very clever and inventive man, known for creating all kinds of brave, new things. In this story alone, he creates a complicated maze and wings for humans to fly with! A labyrinth is often used by writers and artists to symbolise human creativity. Why do you think this is?

Perhaps you can have a go at designing your own labyrinth! It could be winding and complicated, or simple and straightforward. Will there be lots of ways through, or only one?

In this particular labyrinth, a monster is hidden deep inside, so the maze was actually a prison. Can you imagine a creature at the heart of your labyrinth? Perhaps you can describe it to your friends, and if you are a skilful storyteller, you might even be able to scare them!

Daedalus may have been clever, but he was an
unhappy man, and it was his very inventiveness
which brought him the most sadness. Some might
say that this story is telling us something about
the perils of being very clever. What do you think?

The final story is my book is one of my
favourites, and it too tells the tale of a
very creative person. Turn the page to
find out about him and his story...

decem

X

Orpheus et Umbrae

We've almost reached the end of my storytelling, but before I go, there is one final tale to tell about a famous young man. Like Daedalus and Arachne, he has a great talent, but it leads him to a deep, dark place, and a challenge that proves too much for his heart to bear! His name is Orpheus, and we come to this tale just after his wedding to his young love Eurydice.

dum nova nupta per herbas ambulabat, serpentis dente occidit.

vatis Orpheus ad umbras descendit. canem Cerberum vidit, et tum per umbras Persephonen advenit. pulsis ad carmina nervis cantavit: "o dei sub terra. causa viae est coniunx. vipera crescentes annos abstulit. Eurydices, vos oro, fata retegite!
nos omnes vobis venimus, serius aut citius ad unum locum festinamus. haec est domus ultima. non donum sed usum rogo".

Words

So the poet Orpheus sings his pleading song. Will the great gods of the dead listen? Here are the words to help you understand what he sang:

abstulit *from* aufero = *stole away*
ad = *to*
canis (3) = *dog*
cantavit *from* canto (1) = *he sang*
causa (1) = *reason*
crescentes = *growing*

descendo (3) = *I descend*
domus (4) = *home*
Eurydices = *of Eurydice*
fatum (2) = *fate*
festino (1) = *I hurry*
haec = *this*

nos = *we*
nupta (1) = *bride*
occido (3) = *I die*

oro (1) = *I beg*
pulsis ad carmina nervis = *plucking strings to a tune*
retego (3) = *I unravel*
serius aut citius = *sooner or later*

serpentis dente = *from a snake's tooth*
sub terra = *under the earth*
umbra (1) = *shadow, ghost*
usus (4) = *loan*

vatis (3) = *poet*
viae = *of my journey*
vipera (1) = *viper*
vobis = *to you*

Can you pick out an example of a present tense verb, an imperfect tense verb and a perfect tense verb from this passage?

We return now to the deathly silence of the underworld, which has been broken by the strange sound of a living voice, singing out in its gloomy shadows!

tum umbrae lacrimabant. Tantalus undam non
captavit, aves iecur non carpserunt. Sisyphus in
saxo sedit. neque Persephone neque Hades negare
poterant. feminam vocaverunt. illa erat inter umbras
recentes.
unam legem Orpheus accepit ne flectat retro sua
lumina, donec terram advenit.

accepit *from* accipio (3) = *he accepted*

captavit *from* capto (1) = *he captured*

carpserunt *from* carpo (3) = *they plucked*

donec = *until*

iecur (3) = *liver*

in saxo = *on his stone*

inter recentes umbras = *among the new ghosts*

lex (3) = *rule*

ne flectat = *not to turn*

nego (1) = *I say no*

poterant *from* possum = *they were able*

sedit *from* sedeo (2) = *he sat*

vocaverunt *from* voco (1) = *they called*

It probably sounds a straightforward rule, and given he has so much to gain, surely he will be able to hold his nerve on the long, gloomy, spooky journey upwards. What do you think? Let's find out...

Oh, and did you recognise any of the underworld residents?

per longa silentia Orpheus et Eurydice ascenderunt. via
erat ardua, obscura, densa et atra.

non procul abfuerunt. tum Orpheus oculos flexit, et
statim Eurydice relapsa est! lacertos intendens, nil nisi
auras femina rapuit.

Orpheus stupuit. septem dies in ripa sedit. dum vatis
fila sonantia movit, fagus et laurus, coryli et fraxinus,
abies et ilex, platanus et acer, salices et buxum, myrtus
et multae alterae arbores venerunt.

abies (3) = *fir tree*
abfuerunt *from* absum = *they were far away*
acer (2) = *maple tree*

ascenderunt *from* ascendo (3) = *they climbed*
ater/atra = *black*
buxum (2) = *box tree*

corylus (2) = *hazel tree*
densus/a = *dense*
fagus (2) = *beech tree*
fila sonantia = *the sounding strings*

flexit *from* flecto (3) = *he turned*
fraxinus (2) = *ash tree*
hic = *here*
ilex (3) = *oak tree*
intendens = *stretching*

movit *from* moveo (2) = *he moved*
myrtus (2) = *myrtle tree*
nil = *nothing*

nisi = *except*
obscurus/a = *obscure*
oculus (2) = *eye*
platanus (2) = *plane tree*

procul = *far away*
rapuit *from* rapio (3) = *I seize*
relapsa est = *she fell back*
ripa (1) = *riverbank*

salix (3) = *willow tree*
silentium (2) = *silence*
septem dies = *for seven days*
stupuit *from* stupeo (2) = *he was dumbfounded*

Activities

I think we will leave Orpheus to enchant the trees with his grief-stricken song. It's not the end of the story for him, but it is for this little book.

There are so many thoughts that may be going through your mind from this story. Why did he turn back? Why did Persephone and Hades set such a cruel task? Did they intend for him to fail?

I'll leave you to be haunted by all these questions!

I hope you've enjoyed this journey into Latin through these tales of magic, monsters, success, failure, joy and despair.

In my opinion, there's nothing better than a good story, but of course there are some perils in telling tales in Latin.

I should know...

Vocabulary

abfuerunt *from* absum = *they were far away*

abi! = *go away!*

abies (3) = *fir tree*

abstulit = *stole away*

absum = *I am absent/away*

accensus/a = *burnt*

accepit *from* accipio = *I accept/receive*

acer (2) = *maple tree*

ad = *at, to*

addo (3) = *I add*

adhuc = *still*

adsum = *I am here*

advenio (4) = *I arrive at, meet*

aedificavit *from* aedifico = *he built*

aedifico (1) = *I build*

aeneus/a = *bronze*

aer (3) = *air*

aetas (3) = *age*

aestas (3) = *summer*

aeternus/a = *eternal*

ager (2) = *field*

ago (3) = *I do, drive*

ala (1) = *wing*

albus/a = *white*

alterus/a = *other*

altissimus/a = *highest*

amo (1) = *I love*

amicus (2) = *friend*

amor (3) = *love*

ancilla (1) = *slave-girl*

anus (2) = *old woman*

appareo (2) = *I appear*

aqua (1) = *water*

aranea (1) = *spider*

arator (3) = *ploughman*

arbor (3) = *tree*

ardeo (2) = *I burn*

arduus/a = *steep*

argenteus/a = *silver*

ascenderunt *from* ascendo = *they climbed*

ascendo (3) = *I climb*

aspicio (3) = *I look at*

ater/atra = *black*

audi = *listen!*

audio (4) = *I hear*

aufero = *I steal, take away*

augustus/a = *majestic*

aura (1) = *breeze*

aureus/a = *gold*

aures (3) = *ears*

Aurora (1) = *the goddess Dawn*

autumnus (2) = *autumn*
avis (3) = *bird*
axis (3) = *axle*
baculum (2) = *stick*
barba (1) = *beard*
bonus/bona = *good*
brevis/e = *short*
buxum (2) = *box tree*
cado (3) = *I fall*
caelum (2) = *sky*
calor (3) = *heat*
candidus/a = *gleaming white*
cani (2) = *white hair*
canis (3) = *dog*
cantavit *from* canto = *he sang*
canto (1) = *I sing*
capilli (2) = *hair*
captavit *from* capto = *he captured*
capto (1) = *I capture*
caput (3) = *head*
carmen (3) = *song*
carpserunt *from* carpo = *they seized*
carpo (3) = *I seize*
causa (1) = *reason*
cave = *beware!*
caverna (1) = *cave*
cecidit *from* cado = *he fell*

cedo (3) = *I concede*
celo (1) = *I hide*
cena (1) = *dinner*
cera (1) = *wax*
certus/a = *certain*
ceterus/a = *the rest*
cibum (2) = *food*
cinis (3) = *ash*
clamo (1) = *I shout*
clamor (3) = *shout*
collis (3) = *hill*
communis/e = *communal*
congero (3) = *I pile up, gather*
congerunt *from* congero = *they piled up*
coniunx (3) = *wife/husband*
consilium (2) = *advice*
constituo (3) = *I set up*
consumo (3) = *I eat*
corpus (3) = *body*
corylus (2) = *hazel tree*
creavit *from* creo = *he created*
creo (1) = *I create*
crescentes = *growing*
cresco (3) = *I grow*
croceus/a = *yellow*
cum = *with*
cupio (4) = *I desire*
cur = *why*
curro (3) = *I run*

currus (4) = *chariot*
de = *down from*
dea (1) = *goddess*
dedit *from* do = *he gave*
deinde = *then*
deleo (2) = *I destroy*
dens (3) = *tooth*
densus/a = *dense*
descendo (3) = *I descend*
dico (3) = *I say*
diligenter = *carefully*
diu = *for a long time*
do (1) = *I give*
doceo (2) = *I teach*
domina (1) = *mistress*
dominus (2) = *master*
domus (4) = *house,*
  home
donec = *until*
donum (2) = *gift*
duas = *two*
duco (3) = *I lead*
duxit *from* duco = *he led*
ecce! = *look!*
ego = *I*
emitto (3) = *I send out*
equus (2) = *horse*
erat *from* sum = *was*
error (3) = *error*
et = *and*
evanesco = *I vanish*
exclamavit *from* exclamo = *he*
  called out

exclamo (1) = *I call out*
exilium (2) = *exile*
exspecto (1) = *I wait for*
facio (3) = *I do, make*
fagus (2) = *beech tree*
falsus/a = *false*
fama (1) = *fame*
fatum (2) = *fate*
femina (1) = *woman*
fenestra (1) = *window*
fer = *bring!*
ferreus/a = *iron*
fessus/a = *tired*
festino (1) = *I hurry*
figo (3) = *I strike*
filia (1) = *daughter*
filius (2) = *son*
filum (2) = *thread*
finio (4) = *I finish*
finivit *from* finio = *he finished*
flecto (3) = *I turn, bend*
flexit *from* flecto = *he turned*
flos (3) = *flower*
fluo (3) = *I flow*
folium (2) = *leaf, petal*
forma (1) = *shape*
fortis/e = *brave*
fraxinus (2) = *ash tree*
frigidus/a = *cold*
frons (3) = *leaf*
fulmen (3) = *thunderbolt*
fundo (3) = *I pour*
fusus (2) = *spindle*

gaudeo (2) = *I enjoy*

gens (3) = *people*

gladius (2) = *sword*

glomero (1) = *I gather together*

gravis/e = *heavy*

grex (3) = *flock*

habenae (1) = *reins*

habeo (2) = *I have*

habito (1) = *I live*

haereo (2) = *I stick*

herba (1) = *grass*

hic/haec/hoc = *this*

hic = *here*

hiems (3) = *winter*

hodie = *today*

hortus (2) = *garden*

iacite = *throw!*

iacio (3) = *I throw*

iam = *now*

ianua (1) = *door*

ibi = *there*

iecur (3) = *liver*

igitur = *therefore*

ignis (3) = *fire*

ilex (3) = *oak tree*

ille/illa = *he/she*

imago (3) = *image*

imber (3) = *rain*

impello (3) = *I drive*

in = *in/on*

incipio (4) = *I begin*

infirmus/a = *shaky*

initium (2) = *beginning*

innumerus/a = *countless*

inquit = *he/she says*

intendens = *stretching*

intra = *inside*

intravit *from intro* = *he entered*

intro (1) = *I enter*

invenio (4) = *I find*

invenit *from* invenio = *he found*

invito (1) = *I invite*

ipse/ipsa = *himself/ herself*

iratus/a = *angry*

iratissimus/a = *very angry*

ita = *in this way*

ita vero = *yes*

iter (3) = *journey*

iterum = *again*

Iuppiter (3) = *Jupiter*

labor (3) = *work*

labyrinthus (2) = *maze*

lacertus (2) = *arm*

laetus/a = *happy*

lana (1) = *wool*

lapis (3) = *stone*

latus (3) = *side*

laudo (1) = *I praise*

laurus (2) = *laurel tree*

lex (3) = *rule*

ligavit *from* ligo = *he tied*

ligo (1) = *I tie, bind*

liquidus/a = *clear*

longus/a = *long*

ludo (3) = *I play*
lumina (3) = *eyes*
luna (1) = *moon*
lux (3) = *light*
Maeandrus (2) = *the river Maeander*
magister (2) = *teacher*
magnus/a = *large*
maneo (2) = *I stay*
mater (3) = *mother*
medius/a = *middle*
memorabilis/e = *memorable*
mercator (3) = *merchant*
meus/a = *my*
mihi = *to/for me*
minimus/a = *very small*
mirabilis/e = *wonderful*
misceo (2) = *I mix*
mitto (3) = *I send*
modo = *only*
moles (3) = *mass*
mollio (4) = *I soften*
moneo (2) = *I warn, advise*
mons (3) = *mountain*
moveo (2) = *I move*
movit *from* moveo = *he moved*
mox = *soon*
multus/a = *many*
muto (1) = *I change*
myrtus (2) = *myrtle tree*
naso (3) = *nose*
nato (1) = *I swim*

natura (1) = *nature*
navis (3) = *ship*
nec = *nor*
necesse = *necessary*
nego (1) = *I deny*
Nereis = *sea nymph*
nervus (2) = *string*
nil = *nothing*
nisi = *except*
noli = *don't*
nomen (3) = *name*
non = *not*
nos = *we*
nota (1) = *sign*
Notus (2) = *South wind*
novus/a = *new*
nudus/a = *bare*
nullus/a = *no*
nupta (1) = *bride*
nympha (1) = *nymph*
obscurus/a = *obscure*
observo (1) = *I watch*
occido (3) = *I die*
oceanus (2) = *ocean*
oculus (2) = *eye*
oderat *from* odi = *he hated*
odi = *I hate*
olim = *once*
omnis/e = *all*
opis (3) = *help*
oro (1) = *I beg, pray*
orbis (3) = *ball, orb*

ordo (3) = *order*
osculum (2) = *kiss*
paro (1) = *I prepare*
parvus/a = *small*
pastor (3) = *shepherd*
pater (3) = *father*
paulatim = *little by little*
pecunia (1) = *money*
pello (3) = *I strike*
pes (3) = *foot*
penna (1) = *feather*
percutio (3) = *I hit*
periculosus/a = *dangerous*
perterritus/a = *terrified*
pharetra (1) = *quiver*
pingo (3) = *I create a picture of*
piscis (3) = *fish*
platanus (2) = *plane tree*
plaustrum (2) = *wagon*
plumbeus/a = *lead*
pono (3) = *I put, place*
porto (1) = *I carry*
post = *after*
postquam = *after*
posuit *from* pono = *he put*
poterant *from* possum = *they were able*
poterat *from* possum = *he was able*
praeceps = *headlong*
primus/a = *first*
procul = *far away*
pronus/a = *facing downwards*

puella (1) = *girl*
puer (2) = *boy*
pugno (1) = *I fight*
quaerens = *seeking*
quaero (3) = *I seek*
qualis = *just like*
quamvis = *although*
quartus/a = *fourth*
quatio (4) = *I shake*
qui = *who, which*
quis = *who*
quod = *because*
quoque = *also*
radius (2) = *spoke (of wheel)*
radix (3) = *root*
ramus (2) = *branch*
rapio (3) = *I seize*
rapuit *from* rapio = *she seized*
recentes = *recent*
refluo (3) = *I flow back*
regia (1) = *palace*
relabor (1) = *I fall back*
relapsa est *from* relabor = *she fell back*
relinquo (3) = *I leave*
removeo (2) = *I remove*
repeto (3) = *I repeat*
respondeo (2) = *I reply*
retego (3) = *I unravel*
retro = *backwards*
reverto (3) = *I turn back*
rex (3) = *the king*
rideo (2) = *I laughs*

ripa (1) = *riverbank*

rivus (2) = *river*

rogo (1) = *I ask*

rota (1) = *wheel*

rudis/e = *rough*

saepe = *often*

sagitta (1) = *arrow*

salix (3) = *willow tree*

saluto (1) = *I greet*

scio (4) = *I know*

scopulum (2) = *rock*

scribo (3) = *I write*

secundus/a = *second*

sedeo (2) = *I sit*

sedit *from* sedeo = *he sat*

semper = *always*

separo (1) = *I separate*

serpens (3) = *snake*

servavit *from* servo (1) = *he kept*

servus (2) = *slave*

servo (1) = *I keep*

sibi = *to/for him*

silentium (2) = *silence*

silva (1) = *wood*

simulo (1) = *I pretend to be*

sino (3) = *I allow*

sol = *sun*

solus/a = *alone*

sollicitus/a = *worried*

spargo (3) = *I scatter*

spectavit *from* specto = *she looked at*

specto (1) = *I look at*

sperno (3) = *I reject*

stamen (3) = *thread*

statim = *straightaway*

stipuit *from* stupeo = *he was dumbfounded*

stipuerunt *from* stupeo = *they were dumbfounded*

sto (1) = *I stand*

stultus/a = *stupid*

stupeo (2) = *I am dumbfounded*

stygius/a = *of the River Styx*

sub = *under*

subito = *suddenly*

subsido (3) = *I subside*

subter = *underneath*

sum = *I am*

superbia (1) = *pride*

supersum = *I survive, remain*

suus/a = *his, her, its*

taberna (1) = *shop*

tabesco (2) = *I melt*

tamen = *however*

tandem = *at last*

tango (3) = *I touch*

tardus/a = *slow*

tego (3) = *I weave*

tela (1) = *loom*

temerarius/a = *rash*

temo (3) = *pole*

templum (2) = *temple*

tempus (3) = *time*

teneo (2) = *I hold*
tergum (2) = *back*
terra (1) = *land*
tertius/a = *third*
tibi = *to/for you*
timeo (2) = *I am afraid*
tu = *you*
tum = *then*
turbavit *from* turbo = *he mixed up*
turbo (1) = *I disturb, mix up*
tuus/a = *your*
ubi = *when/where*
ullus/a = *any*
ultimus/a = *last*
umbra (1) = *shadow, ghost*
unda (1) = *wave*
unus/una = *one*
urbs (3) = *city*
usus (4) = *loan*
vatis (3) = *poet*
veni = *come!*
venter (3) = *stomach*
ver (3) = *spring*
verbum (2) = *word*
verto (3) = *I turn*
verus/a = *true*
via (1) = *path*
vicit *from* vinco = *he defeated*
victor (3) = *winner*
video (2) = *I see*
vinco (3) = *I defeat*
vinum (2) = *wine*

vipera (1) = *viper*
vir (2) = *man*
visito (1) = *I visit*
vix = *scarcely*
vobis = *to you*
vocaverunt *from* voco = *they called*
voco (1) = *I call*
volo (1) = *I fly*
vos = *you*
vox (3) = *voice*
vulnus (3) = *wound*